Dedicated to
the great Lake
and the
North Woods

Poet Laureate of Duluth

The competition is fierce.
There's the sensuous swell of hills
curving around the city like a sated lover
on the cusp of rekindled desire –
      surely a touchstone for that latent creative fire.

The madcap jesters:
rivers and creeks leaping
      and
            somersaulting
as they tumble and spark their way
through glens and subdivisions,
past parking lots and pristine pines –
      first choice for alliteration and dialectic analogy.

The gulls,
bawdy birds squalling their librettos,
squawking in counterpoint
to the trickster crows
their cries onomatopoeia in motion.

But the front runner unanimously
is the Lake –
that capricious Muse
who takes your breath away
as you crest the hill
and are pierced by moonlight:
      holy reverie.

The restless energy that sails your dreams
      or drowns them.
Unfathomable, yet so intimate
her liquid tongue
flicks the arch of your foot.

Never daily.
She refuses any schedule –
will never flatter fools –
will not chant on demand
or wallow through another wrack
of bloated sonnets.
Neither patience nor praise
are in her lexicon.

But how she sings –
how she condenses sky, rain, dream
into one shining canto
of longing and mystery.

Breathing cloud and thunder,
her magic outstorms any cycle
of rhyme or rhapsody.

Our words are driftwood
tossed on the heat-baked shore,
the scrabbled calligraphy of our
stuttering lyrics
erased by one sighing wave.

Her silence sounds
with metaphor and meaning.
We wait – wordless –
while she tongues the ledgerock,
makes it howl with joy.

Pamela Mittelfehldt

Confluence

you were given to me
          and I to you
your river
falling like breath or light
over stones, airborne
broken silver
          into the river of my own
I hear you falling
through the forest where no one goes
through crimson and evergreen and azure
tumbling in the deep bed
your currents braid with mine
tug upon the roots of things
covering and uncovering
          I take you with
          inside of me
feel your heart frenzy of wings
          reverberating deep tones
for the rain
the sun
the hills fall into us
and rise with a wild sound
weeping and laughing, indivisible

                              Sheila Packa

Rocky Run

Wood floating down a spring freshet,
Red-brown alder and slate-gray sky,
Entangled, wet cedar root...feels good on the foot,
Soft, orange pine-needle bed...Earth floor drum.

                              Mike Nordin

Creek   Cecilia Lieder

Spell

This Spring I cast a spell,
weave a magic prayer for hope.
I place it in a moonlit stream,
light it and watch it move
swiftly down its river road.
The night swallows up my
prayer boat, the light of
my wishes and dreams
passes silently into the void.

All around me in the
radiant darkness, grass stretches,
flowers creak into bud, sap honeys.
All is moving, rustling, restless,
whispering like the river,
busy with life
while my body sleeps,
cold as death.

Only an enchanted kiss
can raise me from this reluctance.

Yet Spring abides.

Cecilia Lieder

Hidden Stuff

Just once I'd like to have a day
to do nothing but watch hawks
and treetop eagles.

Stand by a river when winter melts
and spring flexes her muscles,
the Embarrass or Brule
would do just fine.

Feel the weight of frozen months
rise with the boiling sap steam,
my feet once more anchored
to brown soft ground,
soupstock where ancient elements swim,
hidden stuff of Emerson.

Jan Chronister

Returnings

1.
Salmon rush the stream
into rapids. White wings
of gulls, eagles and ravens
shadow their splashing,
the flash of fins'
riffling circle and streak.

Crowding the bank,
fireweed flare and fume
seed in spinnerets
that drift in swirls of light
on water the salmon
know after years at sea
as source, freshened
sense of even so few
parts per million.

And from millions spawned,
thousands thrashing the gamut
of mouth and gravel.

Like Li Po's poems
set aflame and afloat,
this charged current,
the shallows like
shreds of burning script.

2.
Burning script. How many stories
and the tongues that told them, ash?
Our history, scattered sparks, glimpses.

What had been done to us
we did to each other. Listen

like the blind who must
hear their dreams, these spaces
between our words a distance
we'll cover with our hands.

Survivors to have made it
this far, I reach
for you, here

where we began, are
beginning again, this bed
where we kiss with our eyes open.

Jerah Chadwick

Shore   *Alesa DeJager*

Between two shores

what is the eagle stealing as its long wings grasp and climb

the wind, far up in the silence

with two birds chasing?

On the highway, driving beneath the ascending flights, the
tangling dark birds
in pursuit. Already too late, already the swaying shadows
fail and outwit the tender watch.

What rides on an eagle's indifferent motion

in the rising thermal currents as the sun glances off the wide
surface of the lake,

what waves or sky or emptiness?

What is the news, what wars are beginning
what are the eagles dreaming
as night falls and the cloud's curtain opens on the moon?

What waits in the patterned night

and what wakes to the first light

as streams tumble down the granite faces, break free from
the hill, gain flight
before falling

what are the notes in the birdsong rising and the traffic

what breaks free and is fed
arrives at its destination?

What of the moon shining in broad daylight?

Sheila Packa

And You Say

On the edge
of morning, in those moments
without a name, between darkness and dawn,
after the long night of making love and sculpting tenuous dreams,

we stand naked
at the window and look beyond
the bright incision of horizon, that opening
or ending full of blood and light where water meets sky and we see

the colors
we cannot see, hints of infrared
and infinite, synaptic iridescence from water
to our weary flesh, yearning for wavelengths and light years,

so much
possibility pouring in makes us hard
and wanting each other but we cannot turn away
from the new light lifting and fresh, we stand soaking

our flesh
in the flood of sun and crystal silence
and you say we should walk out on that flaming
path across the water to that place where time is still being born.

Gary Boelhower

Revelation

New leaves, not yet opened, are clenched green fists.
In cloudy inlets, chilled lake air smells sour.
The Coast Guard watchman looks brazen, surly,
Hillside ramparts a backdrop rinsed in rust.
From a low bush, a goldfinch darts, a shock
Of analytical yellow, pure mind.

Not long till the florid months of excess,
With trellised ravines and seared horizons—
After lightning, a pinched, harrowed feeling,
As with journeys planned, but never taken:
The hoped-for revelation does not come,
And the mind sits circumspect, vigilant.

Mark Maire

Slough   *Joel Cooper*

Green

I am the color green
your eyes crave.

Late March,
by now the pines
are insufficient.

I am that half-
remembered-
tender-green,
color of longing

curled in the earth
'til the first inkling
of thaw

asleep in the deep
of a frozen pond,
a promise in my throat

I am on my way to you.

Deborah Cooper

News

where do butterflies sleep
after an all-day struggle
just to stay afloat?

do they rest their weary wings
atop dewy leaves
or rise above it all,
let current events carry them,
destination unknown.

Jane Levin

Camping in Washburn:
no phone, no family,
no crisis— just waves
ringing in. Birds scold,
squirrels gripe, canceling
lunch plans on pinecones.
Woodpeckers drum birch.
The blades of green grass
by my camper wheel
show no need to chat
with distant family
next to the bathhouse;
instead they whisper
amongst their neighbors.
My only morning
chore is another
depth charge, to be drunk
by books stacked on chairs
and binoculars
to watch white boats sail
Chequamegon Bay.

Cal Benson

Firmament

all is permanent
only form changes
waxing and waning
the world turns
inside out over
and over again
drifting in firmament
we cannot comprehend

Donald Dass

Regatta and Blue Horizon   *Tom Rauschenfels*

Regatta

Under the blue water
Over the blue water
The blue sky
There is no difference
We dance across the lake
A ballet of sails
Weaving through each other
Slow adagios
Sudden allegros
As boats move ahead
Fall behind   Each sail
Flying
Through port and starboard tacks
In perfect balance
A leap of the fish
temps de poisson
As they find their marks
Running
To the invisible line of blue
Beyond the blue horizon

Gregory Opstad

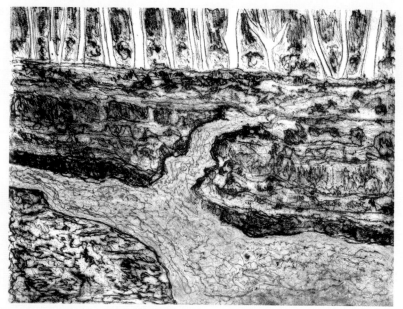

Spring Hike On Gooseberry River

Dark charcoal earth of
sodden river bank punctured
by one bright green shoot.

Filigree branches,
their buds seen in silhouette:
high roost for bird song.

Roaring spring run-off
overruns river's channel,
scours side rocks clean.

Waterfalls rumble
before they come into view:
anticipation.

Ann Niedringhaus

The Cadence of Stone

Along the winding road
heaving through jagged miles
of cut-over pine,
a fox and three kits
tumble on lichen crusted rock.

I stop, roll down the window,
inhale the iron air—
eons of wind and granite—

cut the engine,
and am washed in the
syncopation of centuries,
the steady pulse of stone.

I hear an ancient adagio,
a measured meter echoing
the fossilized flux of time.

Embedded in the archaeology of silence,
the hissing slide of crusting lava stills—
becomes bluff, boulder
cracking under the blaze of sun,
undertow of seasons.

Recalibrate the metronome of memory,
the tempo of the heart:

mossy cliffs begin to melt,
cascading in streams of stone
that pool as gravel,
flashing and spinning—
flinging sparks that dance
as sand.

My pulse slows to the largo of geology,
the ground flows around my feet,
leaps and surges down the riverbed of road.
I drop beside the prancing fox,
riding the cadence of stone.

Pamela Mittlefehldt

At Woodbine Harbor   *Matt Kania*

Joik #9

I perch high
As the eagle
On the craggy tor.

I reach high
As the eagle
Finding the currents of life.

I seek low and high
As the eagle.
There is the past.
And there
is the future.
Above and below.

Katharine Johnson

Perfect Spring

A watercolor fog
smudges us in,
blurring crag lines
with birch and pine,

while waves applaud
their endless delight
at this natural opening.
Fog follows whirling

dervishes of snow
twirling across
the blue ice stage
that broke and plunged

into a forced ballet
of power and line—
choreography that foiled
autumnal projectiles

of red and golden leaves
that twisted and pierced
the wet jazz waves
of a fall quartet.

But now as spring fog lifts
from the lake's stage set,
a woodpecker drums
a syncopated beat

under lithographic
bluestone cliffs
that enclose
this Superior theater.

Cal Benson

Above The Lake

White wisps of eagles' wings and swallows'
tails fly in the cool blue above the lake,
the wide, wise pinions of owls hover,
ghosts of gulls glide, all that is air, light,
feather and filigree, plume and pirouette
through the broad, reaching summer sky.

In these high clouds Jesus speaks of birds
that neither sow nor reap, how every day
we should pour our grief like water
on the thirsty ground and take to flight.
Shake the shackles from our legs, tilt
our faces to the sky-writing clouds and read.

Bones of earth but the air inside whistles
and soars. Flesh that feeds on muscle, power,
wheat and worry; but wide eyes that will not stop
searching the cloud scudded sky. Why try to hang-
on to anything but wonder, anything but wonder.

Gary Boelhower

Unexpected Wonder

I can imagine how it started: unexpected wonder followed
by the desire to preserve it. A meteorologist before weather
satellites, my father photographed clouds. Everyone told him
he was lucky to have "a good job" during the Depression, but
he craved a Divine Call. Climbing up on the airport roof to
pull in weather balloons, he brought along his camera and
tripod. Soon he and my mother were there on the weekends
when conditions were right for specific formations. He
captured a perfect solitary cumulonimbus set in a
pre-storm sky. That image became the trademark for a
marshmallow company. His picture of flat nimbostratus, gray
and knobby, showed an example so average it appeared in
Encyclopedia Americana as visual definition of "cloud." But
the rarest form he recorded was a nameless twisted wisp lying
parallel to the horizon. Apparently unremarkable, it showed
the inner workings of cloud building. Preserved only on our
parsonage wall, whenever Dad explained it, we marveled.

Ann Niedringhaus

Most Unusual Clouds   *Ann Jenkins*

Poem After Seeing Jenkins' 'Most Unusual Clouds'

There are these colors in nature:
the hidden minerals, rock formations
reappearing in gabbro years when
the Spring run-off diminishes

and clay banks of the South Shore
crumble redly into the lake.
The one who had been gathering
agates in the water's edge at sunset

recognizes in the new weather we
first mistook for the good toxic
clouds drifting over the land snagged
by light of the small
hold on permanence of the few.
For only a moment it's felt as
solitude.

Katherine Basham

The Wandering Sky

It's the wind that drives the sky to one side
and herds the stars along, and pulls
the thread out of the needle.
A lifetime frugally spent
but gone all the same, and the chair,
that has become your tame little horse
tethered beneath the wandering sky...
The grandchildren dash through the room
like comets leaving a brilliant trail.
They have left the door wide open
but the wind will close it.

Wherever we go the clouds have preceded us.
Clouds of the vast transformation.
Thin clouds that thinly cross the bald dome.
Clouds like fishbones, like ribs
protecting the lung of the atmosphere.
Sometimes there are long words in the sky,
a sentence finished beyond the horizon.

Connie Wanek

Where There Is No Ocean

Where there is no ocean
sky becomes desire—

we stride its shore,
learn to read the currents,
warn each other of riptides,
the unexpected undertow.

No tables chart the tides of clouds,
mark the neap and ebb
of cumulus, nimbus.

By day
we gaze at the glimmering vastness,
the abyss masked by azure, indigo, pewter—

at night,
we become deep-sea divers
exploring reefs of stars,
gliding past myths and memories
more ancient than Atlantis.

We navigate the clouds,
story the sky with longing—
inhale the saltwind of dawn.

Pamela Mittlefehldt

A Day Like Today

On a day
like today
when the clear syllables
of spring rain sing on the warm
shingles, sudden thunder quickens our hearts,
distant bells ring a muffled melody
through the lazy afternoon,
musty green
moss

on the trunks
of the swaying
cedars shines like the thumb
prints of a God who roams the garden,
whistling, with a hoe propped on his weary shoulder
and promises spilling from his pockets,
when you turn toward me
with your Sunday
smile, your lips

relentless,
your skin tasting
like the everlasting earth,
I can believe the tiny seeds planted
under yesterday's sun soften in their straight rows,
their unbelievable green wishes swelling
toward speech— flower, fruit, seed,
the whole perfect
story.

Gary Boelhower

Fiddleheads   *Joel Moline*

Fiddleheads

Under a canopy of newly leafing trees
The secret world of ferns
Uncoils from the soil's mossy blanket
Hairy claws reach upward
Unfolding themselves
As they stretch into feathery fronds
Gathering motes of sunlight on the forest floor

Susan Niemela Vollmer

Fiddleheads

as if all winter
music was underground

as if the body submerges its rhythms
until snow becomes a memory

and light falls
down into desire
among the mosses
on soft ground into rhizomes

as if
the body could dream
of all the things it couldn't reach

as if first fiddleheads then
root strings
pressed by the fingertips
of everything lost or dead or buried

as if absence drew the bow across shadows
to play a sound
that lifted wings in the branches
and across the breach
springs flow

Sheila Packa

Emerging

The sprout pushes up
corkscrew bent

draws power
from shrunken roots
newly plumped
by rainwater in subsoil

forces excess through striated walls
    into stems
    and leaves
    and tendrils

breaks earth
into chunks

reaches for light
dimly seen
until the last moment.

Then, blinded
as the final membrane
is breached

its push
is doubled by pull
    of light
    and warmth
    and admiration.

Ann Niedringhaus

Black Bird, White Bird
A Meditation on Repinsky's "Untitled"

At first, I thought the dog had caught the little bird, because
she clung upside down to the white pine stump, black feath-
ers ruffled, chirping over and over, as if in pain. But no, she
righted herself and began to drill, hungry. Later, I find her in
the bird book, my first black-backed woodpecker. Next to
the picture, I note the day and place, to annotate someday in
my meager Life List. My mother—the master birder, her title
earned nightly in a murking wood, birdwalking away from
three squabbling daughters and an empty pebbled driveway—
my mother will say she's proud, though through her window in
the dementia ward, she can no longer name even a chickadee.

Later, in the email, a brief note: they've finally moved my
father's files—his aero historian's life work—to the aviation
museum, where his will said it should be. Good. Let them
pore over his faded photographs, his yellowed accounts of
wilderness treks in search of old plane wrecks—especially
the vanished White Bird, a single-engine bi-plane that took
off from Paris on a misty morning in 1927, twelve days before
Lindbergh's spirited flight, but never landed in New York, lost,
some say, in a woolly fog and downed in the Maine woods.
My father, the aero historian, earned his title nightly parked at
the airport, flying away from three demanding daughters and
dogfights in the bedroom, watching the last flight sputter off to
Boston, the drone of its propellers and the din of mosquitoes
indistinguishable as dusk.

Tonight, I look up at the egg-shaped moon—my father dust in
the darkness, my mother bewildered by the light—and marvel
how a black bird, a white bird could bring them back so truly,
their eyes full of passion still fastened on the sky.

Teresa Boyle Falsani

Robert Repinski

Fragile

all of life spills

like egg from shell

golden core

surrounded by mystery

P. A. Pashibin

my love

my love around you is a circle
I wrap you in my blankets
I wrap you with feathers with twigs

with wool I wrap you
with leaves with blues with greens
my love around you is a circle

flights are ways of returning
with silver with russet with crimson
I wrap you with feathers with twigs

let go to fall to the roots
let go to rise in the skies
my love around you is a circle

in sunlight and shadow in music
with scales with flows
I wrap you with feathers with twigs

empty for filling
full for emptying
my love around you is a circle
I wrap you with feathers with twigs

Sheila Packa

During War

The robin appeared one morning at dawn
in the yew bush a foot from our window.
Her nest was wedged between three twigs.

How does she sit so long?

If only she'd leave so we can
see if there's down or chick inside.

There are beaks in the shadow.

Mouths rise up like floodwater
and overflow the brim, reaching out.

When will they fly?

This morning the nest is rent and tipped
with just one neck still craning.
On the ground below lies a tiny leg bone.

Now she's there only briefly.
The small head is quiet.
Then both are gone.

Ann Niedringhaus

Beaver with Branch   *John Peyton*

Redemption

After the Great Flood, *Nanaboozhoo* and four animals floated on a raft
looking for an earth surface on which they could live and walk. *Amik*
(Beaver), *Ojig* (Fisher), and *Nigiig* (Otter) each exhausted their strengths
diving to find where the ground originated, but they were unable to
stay underwater long enough to find the bottom. As they despaired,
the last and smallest animal, *Wazhashk* (Muskrat), asked to take a turn.
Nanaboozhoo and the other animals told him that it was hopeless and
urged him not to try, but the muskrat insisted on doing what he could.
Because of *Wazhashk's* courage and sacrifice the earth was renewed.

Wazhashk, the sky watched this.
Mewinzhaa, long before the memory of mortals,
Wazhashk, the sky watched your timid, gallant warrior body
      deliberate, then plunge
               with odd grace and dreadful fragility
      into translucent black water,
      dark mystery unknown and vast as the night sky
and barely (to a single inhalation shared by a weeping four
and a hopeful splash quieter than an oar) break the surface
      into concentric expanding disappearing rings as
      water circled your departure,
      for a moment transparently covering small soles,
      tiny seed pearl toes
      above that determined small warrior body
      that hurtled from sight then
      in an instant was pulled into cold dark depths,
      seeking the finite in the veins of a waterlocked earth.
Wazhashk, the water covering the earth watched this.
Mewinzhaa, long before the memory of mortals,
Wazhashk, when you were obscured from the sky the water
watched you
      (lost from the sight of the praying four
          alone on a small raft afloat on vast water)

nearly faint under crushing cold
        alone then below the waterline
        seeking the finite in the veins of a cumbrous earth
        as waterfingers intruded and invaded
        all unguarded aspects of your small warrior body
        now stiff and graceless
        pulled by will into icy dark depths.

Wazhashk, in that dark mystery
unknown and vast as the night sky
you continued your solitary plunge
        (lost from the sight of all who lived above water,
                who considered your size and your courage)
until in cold and exhaustion your silent voice whispered

                ninzegizi nigiikaj
                nindayekoz niwiinibaa

                I am frightened I am cold
                        I am tired I must sleep now

and was heard by the Great Spirit.

Wazhashk, you were heard and were answered

                gawiin ni wi maajaa sin
                gaawin gi ga nogan i sinoon

                have courage, have courage in the darkness
                you are not alone, I am always with you
                have courage, have courage in the darkness

'til your spirit roused and spoke

                I hear, I am here, I will try
                through my despair I will

And the Great Spirit watched this and guided you.
Mewinzhaa, long before the memory of mortals,
Wazhashk, the Great Spirit guided you, and watched
        your small curled brown fingers
        stretch curving black claws
                to grasp the muddy, rocky breast
                of a waiting Mother Earth.

And today, Wazhashk, hear us breathe,
our inhalations and exhalations a continuing song
of courage sacrifice grace redemption a continuing song
since long before the memory of mortals.
With each telling of the story with each singing of the song
        we once again rise to break the surface and seek
                the finite beyond the grace of this merciful Earth,
the finite beyond the mercy of this graceful Earth.

                                Linda LeGarde Grover

Black Bear on the Lakewalk   *Matt Kania*

Duluth

"A baby, eh?" That's all he says. She never says he's the father and he never admits it but they get married anyway. This way the city gains another citizen. But for each one that's been born another dies or moves away and things remain more or less the same. The mayor had been dead for several years but he does a better job that way so we keep him in office. We prefer it quiet, understated. At one o'clock Sunday morning the snowplow passes with its flashing blue light and then, ten minutes later, a car, silent, muffled by the snow. That's all. A light still shines in the attic apartment of a large house two blocks away. These old houses, once the mansions of mining millionaires and lumber barons, are full of secrets. Some properties have been completely restored and in others people keep bears as pets. If you are outside around dawn you might catch a glimpse of someone taking a bear for a walk and think, "Why would anyone want a big dog like that? But then…" you say to yourself, "there are all these new people in town."

Louis Jenkins

Musings from Back in the Cave

How embarrassing my barreling
barefoot down Duluth's boardwalk
behind scattering pedestrians,

but I am bored with burrowing
after blueberries and bugs
and campers' deserted Grapenuts

and I am hungry, so hungry
for a deep-fat-fried fellow tourist
that I can hardly bear it.

Strange this boardwalk's bare but for me,
just as I mosey down into town
for its famous summer festivals.

I expected extravagant welcome,
honey suckle and huckleberry blossoms
thrown like confetti from rows on rows

of cheering locals, while I dragged Main
and waved my paws to fair-haired masses,
throwing kisses to pretty mama bears

holding bare-bottomed babies, but I am not
a celebratory bear, no Yogi, Teddy or Smokey;
I am a plain, everyday bear who needs love.

This neglect makes my stomach rumble baritone
grumblings, barbarous confusions between
overbearing expectations and my grizzly gut.

Cal Benson

Wine Cellar in Summer

We open a mossy door to see
pincer bugs skitter for the night cracks
down a cushioned stairwell
creaking warm, fetid
air in billows all around.

The wine cellar
hidden dark and damp
looks alive and a little surprised,
rows and rows of languid bottles
sweating in the rush of warm moist air.
I smile, trace a line on bottle dust,
trace a dust trail on your halflit palm.

Later I know it has been there for years
will be there for years, our bodies
aging with each sip swallowed,
the way a red wine mellows
deep in the belly of earth, deep
in the soul of soil, distilled
beyond the vinegar, the bitter acid dew.

For now, a crimson summer promise,
the warm sweet glow of you
dancing in the heat,
while under skin and deep within,
those damp fragrant bottles
wait until their time again
ripens right.

Teresa Boyle Falsani

Midsummer   *Jon Hinkel*

Fireworks

Black night,
starfish in the sky,
gold chrysanthemums exploding.
Some ignite too soon,
hit Lake Nebagamon with a hiss.
Others linger
leaving smoke spiders that drift away
into the dark,
ghosts of celebration.

Jan Chronister

Bellows of Our Shared Breath   *Nick Wroblewski*

Ikwe Ishiming

From black of light years, *asi anang*
writhed and spiraled into his path,
shedding sparks that dazzled his eyes.
He raised his arm to shade his face
and began his dance, unaware that he danced
while above I flew, gold in the sky.
With my hair the wind I tethered his wrists
to a shining cloud, as I silently swayed
and breathed in the breeze, *ambe, ambe.*
My hands the earth that gave him life
bathed his feet in shedding silk
that tore in my touch as I whispered,
ambe omaa, bimosen, bimosen.
Then my lips rained silver sand that poured
into the river, that rolled from its sleep
and I spoke through the water, *wewiib, wewiib,*
'til he followed, filling my tracks with his own.

Linda LeGarde Grover

Presence

This summer morning is a gift
slowly unwrapping,
pale sheets of tissue paper
carefully folded back
hour by hour as the sky brightens.

Finally the bright present,
a perfect crystal plate.
Ours to break, fill with food,
or set on a shelf in remembrance.
There it will catch the weak, low rays
of January's sun
and give a hopeful glint.

Jan Chronister

Bellows

The clouds rise up,
soft bellows of our shared breath
fan the flames
of the earth's desires.
Red passions burn
where the sky strokes
the horizon.
Every morning
this consummation creates
a new day
into which every living thing
breathes life.
The clouds
whisper stories of everything.
They hint at horses rearing
and whales breaching,
at the big picture
always shifting
in time
to
the steady beat
of
the first prayer—
an almost breathless

yes.

Ellie Schoenfeld

Breathing Peace

Inhalation, exhalation, aspiration, inspiration, meditation
Take it all back to the breath
Consider it now
Either it is only air or something more
The juncture where the soul forms its
State of being; where choices are made
How mindful will we be? How calm?
How open to otherness?
How willing to let the outer state of affairs
Roll past without influence on the inner?
How forgiving will we be? How gentle?

Perhaps it is here in this collective flow of life
That humanity makes its claim on the day

Exultation, song or silence
Gently murmured words of love
Gregorian chants, gospel choirs,
The Buddhist word prayer Om
Breath bolstering the flames of
Kinnickinnic on the native Ossinoggin
All carry the inner self to the outer world
Mingling spirits with the moment
Taking them forth to our chosen gods

If science postulates that human consciousness
Is one facet forming the physicality of time and space
Then let us blow our life force gently
Into the winds of the world
Let our words be spoken like captive
Birds freeing, beating wings against hatred

Take the pause that turns you from judgment
Catch air, gasp in awe
Give yourself a moment's solace to pass
Breath with conscious consideration
Pull the air in deeply, let it settle in
Set your intention for today
Push it all back out, lungs expeller pressed
In this instant be pure, be kind
Each focused breath an anonymous prayer

Lisa Poje Angelos

Sunset on Hale Lake   *Glenna Olson*

Ghost Feathers
(Excerpt)

Without warning, razors spike across Cora's head. Weight forces her fall. Rising from her knees, she braces against confusion. She wills alertness, scanning the haze at the fence-line and tuning her ears to the sounds in the woods. John taught her that, to watch and listen and let the answers come.

The second attack comes with a sound like the riffling of pages, a whoosh that is hardly audible. The sting pierces her scalp. This time Cora drops down hard.

Dazed and shaking, she blinks. For a moment, a silver glow becomes John kneeling on the path. His presence sharpens her awareness to the peeps of the owlets but when she turns her head to find them, John is gone, taking the light. Shadows hide the nest of the Great Gray Owl, the one John called Gray Ghost, the one who takes the raven's home for its own. Cora's fingers dab at the blood in her hair and alone on the trail, she covers her head and waits.

Cheryl Riana Reitan

American Suckers   *Robb Quisling*

D-Con Sonnet Letter

November sixteenth, two thousand and six,
Dear America, I found a dead mouse
by my house's sidewalk, a stiff vic-
tim of D-Con, no doubt, who was doused

with sweetened science, just like Madison
Ave entices our kids to feast—an obese
seeking for diabetes—and to shun
any food not sweet and not dripping grease

soaked bills into superior patriots' tills,
killing sweetly for profit—which is what
brought down the World Trade Towers— chills
predators who want world kids corpulent

and dead. But for profit, so that's ok,
because greed flaunts the American way.

                    Love,
                    Cal Benson

Summer. Central Hillside, Duluth
Even here in this nook of town
heavy with burden and poverty,
we feel the lift of the light,
the elation in the full moon
as it floats huge and pink
over the calm, blue lake.
Finally, after weeks of cold rain and grey
the sun spangles brightly in clear air,
and we all, it seems, let go a little
in the finally warm air.

We're moon-burnt,
lost in pink
and drifting from our cares out
over the great engulfing lake,
infinite, unceasing.

Here, we are spinning
with the pink lake
out into the moon;
drifting in clouds of elation
away from mundane tasks
and the business of life.

Drunk now finally in the spell of light, of green, of warmth;
of a full moon floating over the city
and the earthy summer smell of freshly cut grass.

We're on a summer *uisauniq**,
drifting away from the shore of toil and burden,
out into the moon-drunken zone of summer and light.

Rebecca Vincent

* uisauniq - Iñupiaq word for an ice floe that breaks off with people on it.

The American Way

paying for sex
is illegal
unless   of course
you plan
to tape it   distribute it
make money

Ryan Vine

Cackle of Crows   *Sarah Angst*

Today Show

Blots of ebony perch on nature's ladders,
under twilight skies.
When the frost crack of day breaks,
blots ruffle feathers,
beaks blaring the morning report.

Jane Levin

The murderous crows of London Road

enlist traffic in their treachery.
Two conspirators perch
on wires high above the semaphore.

One measures the patterns
of start, stop, start, dash
triggered by changing lights.

The partner bird keeps a predatory eye
on squirrels intent on being squirrels
among the oaks beside the busy road.

What sparks the synchronized swoop,
the banshee caw that scatters furred creatures
beneath the stealth of outstretched wings?

One squirrel is cut from her path of escape,
forced to the pavement and the precise thud
of her life ending under a wheel.

The crows return to the wire, preen while waiting
for the end of rush hour, the lull that invites
transcendent scavengers to their fresh kill.

P. A. Pashibin

In Defense of Crows

Cathedral ribs rise in ditches.
Crows scavenge carcasses
like shiny robed priests
examining souls.

Purged of fur and flesh,
bones decay.
Death becomes dust
on the deer path.

Jan Chronister

Isle Royale   *Gendron Jensen*

Isle Royale

Since these bones came together,
the presence of silence grows deep,
surrounds and infuses with peace
a powerful dynamic stillness,
thick with wisdom and balance.
A sorcerer's wand has summoned
great spirits from their sleep,
pulling out images that reverberate
a soundless Buddhist gong,
waking the bones of the earth,
who speak to each other again
over the campfire of centuries.

Cecilia Lieder

On Isle Royale

The wolf researcher's yard is littered with bones:
skulls and antlers,
pelvis and jaw bones
and teeth with rings you can count, like a tree's rings,
to see how many summers they've lived.
His wife, Candy, shows us a deformed femur
fused vertebrae
arthritic joints
antlers heavy as stone from marbleized bone disease.
Some poor sot wore these like a cast iron sink on his head —
        for years.
this is what moose do, she says,
they live with pain all the time
they don't complain
they can't do anything about it
they can't take anything for it
you'd think they'd go offer themselves to the wolves,
        but they don't.
they just take it.
Our own lives are all about avoiding suffering and pain,
        she says.
Well, yeah.
But all of nature is about hardship.

It's too bad moose don't write. They would probably make
good poets. If they could find the time for it. Maybe they're
thinking up plots for novels when they're out in the swamp
pulling up water lilies, while the poetry writes itself on their
bones.

                        Margi Preus

Below

May it float underwater,
        may it stay
        submerged —
this news, this loss.

Then maybe
        I can immerse myself
        in my hopes,
never need to emerge.

Below
        edges are softened
        outlines unclear.

In dappled shade
        there is even
        a chance
it has not
        happened at all.

Ann Niedringhaus

Oxbow Lake

How did I get disconnected
And come to be here
Gazing back on youth
From this oxbow lake

My days used to flow
One into another
Like a meandering river
Cutting away at its banks

Donald Dass

Magnetic Moment   *Larry Basky*

Riverside Memories

Daily currents rushed by this place dropping
their random stones. Now slow spinning eddies
hide heavy-weighted particles buried
in sediment. These stones lie scented
with warm body fluids, roughened with coarse
common clay of woodland trail and abundant
backyard garden, brightened with vivid
colors applied in brushstrokes of children's
tempera. I sieve them out, take them
to the brighter light of a forest clearing
for close examination. I roll them
on my open palm. How small these
remnants. How rich their complexity.

Ann Niedringhaus

Dancing children, leaping like goats
across Lake Superior's rocky beaches
pausing for striking moments
to shoot their tooth-pocketed chewing
gum through the sunshine.
Then pauses the magnificent arch
which ends with a light click
as it melts with lapping waves,
stretching and assimilating
into the lake over time
like a boy sucking blood from a wound.
The cycle continues, and always will.
Over time, the gum will release
and lose itself combining
with the shifting waters,
on another slowly worn rock
at the bottom, as it is accepted.

A glimmering string of marble reflections
stretching with aching and quiet need,
creeps down honey like tears,
toward the reflected
dirty child's face.
In one moment
the string snaps
and bursts ecstatic pearls
falling gently after coalescing
in mid-air, kerplunking
and into the trembling place.
The boys leap back to their
parents full of emotion.

Peggy Anderson

Magic Moment   *Betsy Bowen*

Perhaps Love

He is the one who sits with me at sunset
I am the one forever by his side

We want our rightness
to hold the world together
everyone in place

Perhaps love
is just another word for linger

P. A. Pashibin

The Waves

And the days spent with you
One
Overlapping the next.
Then,
just often enough,
a bold one
makes its move,
rinses
away the grit
leaving something shiny.

Candice Richards

Evening Sky on the North Shore   *Ann Jenkins*

After Thirty-five Years

At first, it's true, I was bewitched by you
You're beautiful, but rough around the edges
You think you're such a bigshot, always bragging:
"The biggest and the deepest and the cleanest."

But now, a lot about you bothers me:
Communication's always been a problem
You only groan and grunt, making hissing sounds
And, really, I can never count on you
One minute gentle, the next gray and sullen
And sometimes downright mean:
you've cut and bruised me
Your temper's bad, your disposition's cold
And still, you think you're, well, Superior.

My old boyfriend back East beguiles me still:
He's smooth around the edges, fine and soft
He can be stormy too, but every night
He reaches out to me, wave after wave
His tears salty, as tears ought to be
He buoys me up when I am feeling low
Then rocks me as he gently cradles me
He's my first love. I'm tempted to return.

Mara Kirk Hart

Lake Superior Horizon

Suppose you drag a paintbrush, soaked with gray
acrylic, straight and fast across a canvas
barely skimming the gessoed surface. Setting
that line decides it: the captured day
will not be one of earthbound fog. Gone too
the possibility of encroaching shoreline
and rising hilltop shadows, all gone
with the flick of your wrist. Place
your horizon too high and there's no room
for the protean clouds, the starring actors.
Going on to make all those small choices
of color, stroke and shape, you suspend
in place what is moving before me.
Suppose you stop with that line.

Ann Niedringhaus

53

Lake Superior

Days on end this lake is a gray
lady of grief, lifeless and brooding,
sighing a litany of lamentations.

And other days she's sparkling, sequined
every color, shining silver and jewels,
a soaring descant of desire.

Perhaps she mimics us, no more or less
than a mirror for our most extravagant
longings and our unfaithful despair.

But not our mirror alone, come the dawn,
she takes the light and oh the dance she does,
she lifts the light and shakes it,

her whole body shivers and delights,
every fluid syllable filled with luminescence,
every cell a refraction of praise.

Gary Boelhower

Summer Day, Submerged

Along the trail above Meyer's Beach I say good-bye
to what
rises and illuminates, then shifts and falls away

like the day
in my kayak, I paddled toward the sea caves but the waves
drove me back

to shore to comb the beach and walk along the path
up and down
the hills to the precipice to watch the boats below flow in and out

of the caves.
Either we gaze from high or try again the vessel or swim in it or
drown the beauty

or danger where each tiny cupped surface pans the sun, catching
like a star
that falls into a sea of stars.

Sheila Packa

Split Rock　　　　　　　　　*Joel Moline*

The Lake Remembers

Before the icon
When the beauty of the cliff alone
Stole breath away
There was already a story here
Many fires lit along the curving shore
Sweet non-fern, cedar and bearberry
Carried in smoke sweetly scented
To the mystery of God and ancestors
Hands set to good work
The gathering of birch for baskets
Bone needles punching through hide
Trips to the island for berries to dry
Not for campers' pleasure, but for life
Small blue spheres holding promise
Of the slow hard walk into another Spring

Lisa Poje Angelos

Blue Eden

When my two children were spending their summers in Duluth, when they were old enough to be away from me but not old enough to leave our street, they would escape to our neighborhood wilderness, Blueberry Hill. On summer days once school let out, the sisters would climb the back side of the hill where there was just a hint of trail to find their own blue Eden. How many things I do not know about those hours!—but this I can report: they picked handfuls of wildflowers blooming in batches of yellow, orange and blue; they ate bunches of blueberries, small, round and squishy. From high on the hill they looked down on the deep blue lake and then up at its sister in the sky. In those sweet blue days they didn't see any clouds at all and, even though I should have known better, neither did I.

Lezlie Oachs

Shortcut

Late in June
newborn blueberries
greet the moon
where Bayfield's ridge
descends into Chequamegon.

Across the Battleaxe
we pass backdoor roads
to secret lakes and Herbster,
turn toward Tripp,
bouncing over soft sand,
once Superior's south shore.

Welcomed by hayfields,
we reach our ballpark destination,
north of Harry's Corner,
clouds a checkered turtle's shell,
porcelain sky an Oulu blue.

Jan Chronister

Bunches of Blueberries   *Sarah Angst*

Superior Trail

Piney paths,
where blueberry dots wink
engraved invitations
and birches impersonate chickadees
   performing improvisational arias
pitch perfect.

Jane Levin

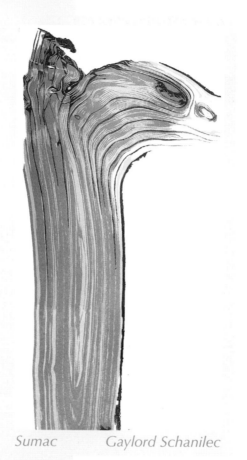

Sumac   Gaylord Schanilec

Watching

The sunlight charms the leaf
out of its bud.
Pale green luminous cobra
with a walleye on its back,
it watches
the orderly and the unorderly world
laid out at its metaphorical feet.
It slithers and swims into the light.
It dances to the music of the sun.
It keeps its eyes on something
not yet seen.

Ellie Schoenfeld

Several Dozen Shades of Green

Down here in the ravine, we have the model
By means of which the sad United Nations
Might actually succeed: Every species
Flies its own peculiar flag –
Raggedy valerian, broadleaf maple,
        pom-pom of the pine,
The ferns unfurled, tassels of the grass,
And the willow drags its drooping
        pennant in the water.
Each declares, defiantly, its own identity,
All compete for space and spread and height,
And yet they've all agreed somehow
To work together for the greater good of green.
And aren't we lucky things turned out this way?
What if leaves had been taxicab yellow
        or, worse yet, dull as mud?
Think how jumpy we'd have been
        or seriously depressed!
Instead we are soothed and encouraged by green,
        made semi-serene,
At least for a season, though those of us
        who walk here in December know
This great glorification of chlorophyll,
        these snowflakes formed of cellulose,
This crisscross reach and rush of vegetation
        is just a passing dream.

Barton Sutter

Protest Poem

Joan Baez sits in a tree
in a park somewhere
to raise awareness of
Joan Baez sitting in a tree
in a park somewhere.

Ryan Vine

Late September

The cabin whistles *hurry up,*
bring everyone, I've room enough.
We fill the trunk with sweet corn and brats,
cases of Summit, it'll be hot.
Speeding north on I-35,
counting the hours 'til we arrive.

A Hinckley stop for Tobie's treats,
bathroom break and a quick retreat.
At Skyline Park, excitement mounts,
Duluth is close, that's all that counts.
We crane our necks, ready to brake,
when the youngest shouts *there's the lake!*

Up 61, with no delays,
Tofte, Lutsen, we're home - Cascade.
Kids scramble out, run to the shore,
then disappear, off to explore.
Mothers unload into the frig,
head for the cedar, 'cross the bridge.

Dinner is a casual affair,
fingers, not forks - nobody cares.
Soon all that's left are buttery globs
and mountainous piles of well-gnawed cobs.
Empties litter the screen porch floor,
for dessert - Betty's pies and s'mores.

By ten, winking fireflies delight,
the sky swirls green with northern lights.
I want to stay here forever,
family, friends, we're all together.
But frosty air nips at my toes,
whispers, *It's almost time to close.*

Jane Levin

Cascade Cabin   *Joel Cooper*

Stones

You keep a stone from the island
in your pocket,
hold it in your hands like a prayer,
place it under your pillow
like a talisman
who whispers stories to you in the night.
You keep one in your pocket
and under your pillow
until that day arrives

when you leave it
on the hearth
and walk out the door
for the final time.
You take one last look around
before you cross the hidden bridge
on the other side of the island.
You cross that bridge
which no one can see with these eyes
but which the rocks
have been quietly describing to you for years.
Your last breath here is
a sigh of relief,
a smoky prayer the stones taught you
while you were sleeping.

Ellie Schoenfeld

Tucked away in a book in the cabin
To Karla

In the quiet of my days,
　　You are here.
In fantasy and image,
　　We speak and touch.
Reality diminished, and yet… more real.

For here there is no monstrous lie
　　That love destroys,
No heartless rule,
　　That intimacy be bound with shame.
Here… Love need not be earned,
　　May not be owned,
　　　　Is not denied.

A child's world regained.

Where honesty and love go hand in hand,
　　… Feeling and knowing are clean and undefiled,
　　　　… Yesterdays are put away,
　　　　　　And tomorrows wait their turn.

I come here more often now,
　　And bring with me ones I love.
Sometimes I stop halfway between,
　　And wonder… Which is reality?
　　　　… Which the dreams?

Marsh Ward

West Entrance   *Gordon Manary*

Sunday Night

Taconite cars interlock with a thud,
And the leaves on nearby trees show silver
In the updraft. Clouds scud the horizon.
Seagulls swoop in taut semicircles.
The freeway streams headlong, beam after beam.
In tall houses, windowpanes flash and glint
With strange shadows and afterimages.
Enormous worlds are put back on high shelves,
Crucial objects slid back into drawers:
The week a wound we dress, undress, dress again.

Mark Maire

Circle the Wagons

Setting sun
on our westward road
sends an arrow shaft
straight as Stonehenge,
knife-slicing a cleft
through thick forest.

Blaze of maples
brings no consolation
when we round the corner
to winter.

Circle the wagons,
light the fires,
prepare for a siege of darkness.

Jan Chronister

Compassion   *Cecilia Lieder*

Autumn

That day hangs out intense
Along the sky and will not let go.
It moves around my heart
Humming and stirring up the air
Glowing out like coal fire
Bright against dark memory.
Instants keep returning
To flame up and out again in joy.

Cecilia Lieder

Nothing Says North

Nothing says north like a white pine
Unless it's a maple gone red to maroon
Except for the way cedars lean from the shoreline
Nothing says north like a white pine
But birches so bright that they shout about sunshine
And then there's the tamarack's gold in the gloom
But nothing says north like a white pine
Unless it's a maple gone red to maroon.

Barton Sutter

The Gleaner

Ducking twigs from last storm's fury,
Deer paths guide through seasoned wood.
Clinging bedstraw wraps my ankle,
Balsam down, where once it stood.

Rotting logs embraced by birch bark,
Wild mint bruised assaults my nose
Burrs and ticks hitch rides on pant legs
Forest flotsam freely blows.

Plucking Pearly Everlasting,
Willows weep and poplars sigh.
Vines and ground-pine duck for cover,
maples bow as I walk by.

Fleecing rocks of moss like velvet,
Balconies of fungus, torn.
Basket filling while I plunder
Rubbish from the forest floor.

Candice Richards

Compassion

Beauty and pain
are one.

Great moments
of joy
ache inside
and resonate
the deepest realm
of tears.

The line of a petal,
pure and perfect,
hurts the eye
that worships it.

And the scent
of life
obliterates
my being
into resinless
ecstatic
shatter.

Beauty and pain
are one.

Cecilia Lieder

Not Singing

Because the heart
is a fist
in the closet of the chest,
a shut-away tapping,
and pounding more
easily ignored
than deciphered.

Because the body
is a burnished door,
our revolving
admission and refusal.

Because we often
enter and go
no further than the first
few steps, eyes closed
in familiar fear,
that dark we have
no need for words to.

Jerah Chadwick

What We Don't Know Will Save Us

Two months without rain, but still the stream,
Reduced to a rill, sends a white streak
Down the rock and then meanders darkly down
The watercourse, a musical trickle that bubbles and slips
Gradually downhill, yearning toward the lake.
The leaves have curled and turned before their time,
The path is dusty dry, and yet the water runs.
There must be sources underground that we don't know about.

Else why, in those sleepwalking weeks you eased
        your husband toward his death,
Did you wake from an orgasmic dream about
        a dark-haired man you'd never met?
Else why, when you were young and
        thrilled by swirling crowds,
The glinting stone and glass, the foreign accents of the city,
Did you dream a quiet village where
        everything was made by hand?
Else why, in those years your daughter called you
        hateful names each day
And pushed you over in your chair so that
        you looked up boarding schools
Did you glimpse a black-toothed woman
        who snarled behind her shopping cart
And guess that you might gut it out
        for one more shell-shocked month?
There must be sources underground that we don't know about.

Barton Sutter

69

Confession 　　　　　　　　　　　　*Anna Marie Pavlik*

Thief

My headlights wobble on the water's surface
as I drive at night along a riverbed,
deep in an unmapped world of inner rain.

In windows of strange houses, lights flicker
through trees, heralding someone else's fame.

In the shoals, there is the graduated
wearing away of all that vanishes.

If a new day dawned, its sun would sear my tongue
into a thin pink flame. It would scorch my heart
to a pile of ash blue as poison.

Dazzled, my eyes would be pinned wide open.
Yellow thief, it would burn down my house,
and cauterize all that I have lost.

　　　　　　　　　　　Mark Maire

Confessional Poem

I never told him anything
he didn't expect—
the white lies of a small girl,
a week's accumulations
related in halting, mouse-like whispers.
He blessed me anyway
and gave me my penance
and bid me go in peace.
Perhaps the next penitent
would offer him what he came for,
a great, meaty, mortal sin like adultery
described in gorgeous language,
words that lit up the confessional
like a flashlight in a closet:
a silk cuff missing its button,
sheer stockings coiled on the floor,
shoes with heels like wine glass stems—
the hypnotic black and white images of film noir,
wherein all eyes followed a bad star
with uncontrollable longing.

Connie Wanek

Last Wishes

Drag me out in the woods
when I die.
Let eagles guard my carcass.
Let foxes and fishers
tear my flesh,
carry bits back
to burrows
to feed their kits.
Let my spirit ride
on the wings of raptors,
defying decay,
needing no resurrection.

Jan Chronister

Shadow in the Twilight

In the twilight of forest
in layers of shadow
where limb tangles with limb
I follow a shadow of another kind

under ash trees, inside leaf
green spheres, under fallen
trees with crowns touching ground,
around upended roots,

through dark trunks,
over streams flowing
and dreams
down toward the river

follow without knowing
what I follow that falls
over stones
into caverns, around hidden turns,

that divides itself into two or three
and joins into one, goes deep.

Sheila Packa

Joik #8

I am alone.
No home fire to comfort me.
Mosquitoes hatch in the bog.
Beavi spreads her rays day and night.

The goose tends her brood.
I have left my family.
No one tends to me.

Mother fox watches as her kits stray
Further from the den.
Playful and curious.
No mother watches as I stray
Further from my people.

When I am tired and hungry,
I scratch the thin soil of this earth.
I suck the dry rocks of this land.
I curl upon mosses and leaves.
In this wilderness of beauty,
I am alone.

Katharine Johnson

Red-tailed Hawk   *Alesa DeJager*

Red Tail on Low Wire

earth-brown, hunched statue
stark reversal and mute sentinel
misplaced a scant yard and a half
above the amber wayside weeds
crushed cans, bits of glass,
and crisping uncut grass

reason and years of upturned gazing
suggest he should be higher up
on daily watch from yardarm
treetops, weathered poles, or
convenient garish billboards alert
for luckless rodents or road kill

razor eyes like high-powered scopes
scan their snow-blotched killing ground
a fifty-foot lessening of his customary perch
increases his odds, levels the field,
pulls the random asphalt crossings nearer
makes his hovering ballet more brief

transfixed, immobile talons grip
the frozen fencepost while his
subtle canny tilt and raptor-born death stare
are a chilly monument to adaptation
witnessed by few who speed blithely past
this stark reminder, this roadside still life

Phil Fitzpatrick

A Time of Fire   *Kurt Seaberg*

To the Past Seasons of My Mind

In the seasons I have known you...
        I have shared you over and over in
        my mind
... with the first cold snowball thrown
        in winter's flurry among the blue and
        white thoughts
... to the arm and arm embraces of
        spring's cleansing of the soul full of
        after thoughts
...from the hot sticky rapids of
        your summer body exhausted from
        activity
... to the ending of summer's havoc
        to the falling leaves that crunched
        beneath our beings.

My mind aches over and over for
        you
... for each revibration, the struggle
        is long within me.

To the seasons I have known you...
... yet, you haven't the will to
        call back a single season of our
        life as the seasons pass on and on.

Peggy Anderson

Fire

Strange
that after all those years
of terror before loneliness,
now that it has come
I have no fear.

It was never the loneliness
that was fearsome;
it was the loss of you,
of the flame between us.
Now that it is gone,
there is nothing left to fear.

Somewhere along the hard path
that we have walked together,
you veered off
to a road I could not walk.
Or would not.

With ruthless fire
you charred the ground
between us
killing the connecting flame
lest I follow you
too far.
Lest you too

become fire.

Cecilia Lieder

Chorus   *Joe Furuseth*

Wood Frogs

You couldn't have heard
this chorus of clay colored
buddhas, pale stripes down
their backs, in water looking
exactly like stones, this chorus
of scat singing males like this
was a street corner in Boundary
Waters, this raccoon faced
chorus clacking like ducks
you wouldn't have heard
if you hadn't landed the canoe
against a deadfall, cattails, and
laborador, this island of one white
pine and three jacks, looking for
what? Blueberry blossoms
you couldn't have heard.

Jim Johnson

Autumn

Like Keats, I welcome Autumn this year,
having spent the summer watching my father die,
his limbs waste and wither slowly,
eyes cloud the sun,
voice fade to silence,
heart slow to final freeze.
Now, come November, a replay all around me.
Sugar maples wave their scrawny hands,
garden and grasses bend to grovel
like supplicants,
the peepers' wailful chorus quiet in the reeds.
Frost creeps like mold in the hollows,
ice on the lake reflects indifference in the sky.

Come, bleak November.
Do your worst.
I can live buried in snow,
get along without green,
even eye with gratitude
your weak deceitful sun,
the way we learn to carry on
in this diminished world
without our dead.

Teresa Boyle Falsani

Connection

Hello? Hello, the man with the cell phone says,
spinning around the restaurant.

He's lifted his elbow
above his shoulder, little flag of himself,

his blank phone
to his ear. Hello? Hello?

Hello, the seated people, as he passes, say and raise
their heads from grazing. Hello?

Ryan Vine

Reliquary   *Anna Marie Pavlik*

What Is Holy?

Peering through the glass coffin at the relic Saint who was
Clothed in garnet brocade with filigreed golden thread
And lain eternally still on a lustrous white satin pillow
Hand embroidered with the lily of purity
I've wondered

At Chartres passing over the labyrinth on which
So many suffered for their journeys and their quests
Pausing at the Sancta Camisia, ancient cloth that
Wrapped the Blessed Virgin in palest yellow
I've wondered

Coolly moving through churches in Spain
Lingering at the collections of golden and crystalline frames
Almost obscenely celebratory in their stemmed housing
Of a single thorn, a scrap of wood, a bone
I've wondered

What is holy?
How are pilgrims inspired to see God?
Journeying for days to lie prostrate at the reliquaries
They show their faithfulness in the presence
Of a bit of the cross, a piece of the body of their
Sacred martyr, a shock of hair, a garment

Beyond all I've wondered what of the earth that fed
their sacred one; the clear flowing water that quenched thirst?
Why not the swaying cattails of the marsh, the songs of
Birds beyond the most angelic of choirs
For their pilgrimages and their funds?

Not worthy of the sacrifice or the offerings of the masses
The wetlands today have come to be storehouses of
The relics of the natural and wild balance of a lost earth
Perhaps if we can find the holiness in the fragments
We will have our miracles and our grace

Lisa Poje Angelos

Raking Leaves

Hurried by a warm all-hallow's wind
I comb grass like a mortician.

Dry leaves embalmed on damp moss
have said good-bye to their birth tree.

Last rites of raking
bury them
in a windless grave,
to be reborn
in bird bellies and April buds.

Small brown fragments
like pottery shards
stick to my socks
and fall inside my shoes.

I find them at night
on my bedroom rug,
pieces of eternity's
parchment map.

Jan Chronister

Midwest Prophecy

Taconite to their hatches
ore boats still float. Rusty red
thousand footers float too
concrete full. Soon steel
and concrete float as skyscrapers
on some horizon. Some country
boy sees them shimmering
in their coats of glass.
Through the front window
of his mother's car—all
they own backseated, trunked
in bags and boxes—he watches
in wonder them breach
the ground before him and swell
with sky. He touches his ear
to the side window. He hears
the vague tethers snap.

Ryan Vine

Sanctuary

Right here in this small
bright clearing among
the reaching emerald branches,
I plant my heart like the seed
of everything possible, everything
to hope for, to believe in.

Right here where the sweet
sweat of earth rises from this mulch
of moss and decaying needles,
from this mix of shit and stardust,
and mingles with the stinging scent
of pine. The tall trunks sway
like the hot hips of God in their
birthing dance and the vital
vernix of spring seeps from
every pore in the warming bark.

This is the Eden of desire, the genesis
garden where a heart can break
open like a promise, where a body
can stretch its endless longings
and trust the river of its own blood.

This is the original story, before
the tree of knowledge, before we made
the jealous gods in the image of our
fears, before the curse of shame.
This is the garden of grace, the long
sigh of belonging, breath of home.

Gary Boelhower

In Winter

The sun slips out early.
Trees release
their long blue shadows
in the snow
and dream of leaves
and feathers.

Everything softens
in this hour,
the light outside the windows
and the light behind our eyes.

We lay the fire
and find our ways
to keep each other warm.

Deborah Cooper

So Much Light

Through sky blue windows, we saw steep white hills.
A road, bleached with winter salt, led uphill.
Between tamaracks, shadows were violet.

Below, twin bridges glittered in noon sun,
On either side a miniature city
Dotted with amethyst basilicas.

So much light made us giddy, indifferent:
We hedged all our debts, plotted the future,
Wrote off the vanished possibilities.

A marvel in intemperate latitudes:
First green shoots, the resuscitated heart,
A man suddenly wanting his life again.

Mark Maire

The Luminous Hour   *Kurt Seaberg*

I am waiting,
like the Spring.

Outside, the snow
counts coup
on my dreams of
green growth

but inside
I fan tiny sparks
in the dark
and pray,
worshipping hope.

I guide the stranger
to the fire's warmth
and call him God.

                    Cecilia Lieder

The Luminous Hour

There is the light within the tree,
within all the trees,
and upon the fresh snow that blankets
the earth from winter's cruelest tempers.
In the first light a single stalk,
the remains of summer's yarrow,
looks around to see what else
has not been buried by the night's addition.

Micky McGilligan

Spring Break

After twelve hours of blizzard
the trees out back are
coming into focus.

In oversized boots
I trudge out to the garage
retrieve food from the freezer;
sturdy kernels of corn
glow like tiny turbans
possessing secrets.

I would not replace powdery snow
with golden pollen or
stiff frozen birch with
crackling cornstalks.

Confined like a monk,
I grab blanket and books,
enjoy my silent cell.

Jan Chronister

Taking Off!   *Beckie Prange*

Dissociative Fugue

We could run away, maybe even fly
down to some little Mexican town.
We'll set up camp on the edge of nowhere,
los gringos con nada perder so we're safe
from bandits or identity thieves on both
sides of borderline and we'll just live live live
wrapped in sun yellow
mellow mango

or

We might stay in these cold Minnesota bones,
lock ourselves in shivers deeper than
Lake Superior blue, hungry
for fire, brimstone, baptism
whatever it takes to burn our names boldly
into our darkened coats, as we prance
like *conquistadores*, braced
for the onslaught of one
Alberta Clipper

P. A. Pashibin

Winter Moon   *Ann Jenkins*

Blue Moon

The moon looks worried, rising above the Lake. The moon looks so unhappy, so pale. The moon has not been well. The moon has had a lot of problems with meteors, especially in youth. And night after night, the same earth rises . . . It hasn't been easy for the moon. The moon . . . The moon . . . The moon this and the moon that. You drive faster but the moon keeps pace, looking sadly into your car window. "Why are you leaving," the moon wonders, "and where will you go?"

Louis Jenkins

Twelve Tone Geese

in synchrony and angles

across forests over rivers

below Venus

clouds invisible borders

carrying nothing

besides star memories

besides starred memories

along the arteries of the body

into dark interiors

through the moon's phases

calling to each other over

lovers' endless roads

Sheila Packa

Life in Oulu

In 1926
every forty acres
a homestead;
mailboxes read like
Finland's map,
Wentala
Yrjanainen
Rantala
Suihkonnen,
neighbors offering
placenta pudding
pickle recipes
over strong coffee
in the basement of the
Lutheran Church.

Potluck   *Diane Chaney*

Before they closed the co-op
you could buy big boxes of matches
cheesecloth by the yard
milk filters
aluminum funnels
kerosene,
listen to Reino's bobbing conversation
with first generation settlers.

Elm trees that once roofed pastures
are gone,
anguished limbs piled like Holocaust bones,
hayfields surrender to popple,
orchards retreat to weeds.

Tall frame houses close their eyes,
fall down in sleep,
sweet-filled barns and midsummer fires
a forgotten dream.

Jan Chronister

Potluck

The Church of the Twelve Holy Apostles
Chicken Dinner

Sitting across the table in
The Church-basement din
Watching her greased lips
Spill baklava and
Tales of barefoot saints

Miracles
Martyrs
Relics
Young girls
All gloriously
Dead.

The soft scapula around her neck tangles,
Jumps from her sweater
While her words leak and pool
Till talk of retreats
And Carmelites
Become a flood
As she parts the sea of gravy with her soft white roll.

A life of prayer
And study
Following the barefoot Saint
On the high, rigid line
She has learned to walk the rope,
And needs no net
Her universe perfectly aligned.

Candice Richards

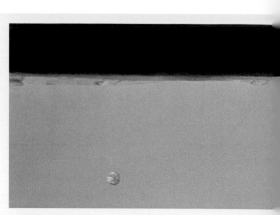

Reflections on the Moon

Grown Children

The full moon wakes the eldest son
on his makeshift cot in the living room.
You can sleep when you're dead, it says.
It's making good time across the sky
in spite of the wind,
like a car driving all night to cross the plains
ahead of the snow.

The grown children have returned in time
to say good bye to their mother.
It's like Thanksgiving or Christmas,
cars parked on the lawn,
the little house so full. Early and late
lights are on; they feel guilty sleeping
or smiling or eating, rummaging
through her kitchen, observing
her needless frugality, cheese wrapped
in the lining of cereal boxes,
the freezer burning her day old breads.
Between hospital visits they rake and chop wood
and keep the bird feeder full.

Who feels it most?
Who puts the coffee on at 3 a.m.?
Soon there will be no parent to shield him.
The curtain will open
and he'll be standing at the picture window
where anyone or anything might see him,
his silhouette, holding his hot mug, waiting
for the inevitable celestial evidence
that day will come.

Connie Wanek

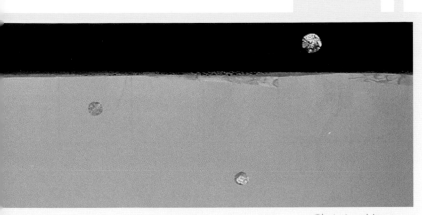

Christine Herman

The Stone

Just in case I cannot sleep
I keep the smooth stone
on the table by the bed.
Even in the dark
my hand can reach it
without stumbling.

This is a stone which I believe
traveled a great distance
to find me on the shore.
It fits perfectly
in the shallow bowl
of my right palm.

The stone is the color
of the night sky
and inside it
floats a tiny moon,
whole and silent.

I can feel it shining
in my hand,
along my arm,
into my shoulder
and I sleep.

And when I wake
at the alarm
I feel as if I've come
from far away,
across the dark arc
of the sky.

Deborah Cooper

Story Hunger
—After the Irish

Whether for seal or shark oil
or tallow, the lamp, too,
a hungry mouth. How its wick

cast the room through
winter nights: faces gleaming, bodies
leaning from the shadows as if

from just below the surface.
Outside, wind, the restlessness
of water, breaking

or raging storm. Think
of the table's patient stance,
something to chew

off little bits of winter,
dark held like a wafer
at the center of the flame.

Who would taste
the light's portion took blindness
on his tongue. Who starving would eat

grasped as the drowning do,
danger to whatever could be.
And our bowls' emptiness,

the way imagining sets
off stumbling
land legs of a possible world.

Jerah Chadwick

Midwinter's Evening   *Jim Meyer*

After the Blizzard

I am standing under a canopy of emerald
branches mounded with snow. Moon light
filters through and then comes the silence,
deeper than secrets, deeper than the words
that can't be said, deeper than the nagging
doubts that chatter behind my eyes.
This is the silence of moonlight
on snow drifts and I am content
to stand here breathing like a baby just born.

Gary Boelhower

95

This Stillness

thing about the play of winter's light
A fragile delicacy amidst the harshest cold
Painting its daily masterpiece in muted hues
Of plum and apricot upon the idle snow

There is something about the purity of silence
A transitory space between the bitter winds
Hanging poised among the burdened boughs
As pensive as your breath yet unreleased

Pause here and find some ease against struggle
With all the vibrant distractions of boisterous green
Laid low, all the summer humming hushed
Allow yourself too a dormancy

This stillness of air, this stillness of mind
This clarity cannot be found
On any night in June

Lisa Poje Angelos

The Plot against Juhannus Juhlat

Less than two months shy of solstice
snow covers the ground,
glowing in late daylight
like clean sheets.
Lacy ice edges evergreen gowns
just in time for high school proms.

One more storm,
one last slippery road.
In my car I play the blues,
there's nothing else to do.

Jan Chronister

Nindaaniss Waawashkeshii-Kwesens
On a Winter Night

In the moonlit quiet of a winter night
as I pass her bedroom door
Nindaaniss Waawashkeshii-Kwesens
my daughter the Deer Girl
springs from her bed.
While in startled graceful silence
she totters to my arms,
from the distant dark forest of her sleep
her wide dark eyes ask "What? *Wegonen?*"
and I carefully lead her back to her bed.
"My girl, sh, sh, *niibaan, niibaan,*
go to sleep, go back to sleep."
Folding her long legs beneath herself
she nestles under the pile of blankets
I tuck around her
and her wide dark eyes close
as she returns to the distant dark forest sleep
of the *Waawashkeshiiwug.*

Linda LeGarde Grover

Midwinter's Evening

Between the flowing branches of the white spruce
And the gray water lapping against the rocks

The only sound is the cacophony of ducks
As they huddle beside the iced-over bay
The sun fades to pink streaks
A misshapen moon wanders overhead

It casts our shadows in brief silhouette
Fleeting slivers in the close of this day

Susan Niemela Vollmer

Spruce Swamp Sunset   *Tom Rauschenfels*

Late Winter Day

At last, the sun succeeds...

wearing a hole in the fabric
that drapes the sky.

I am waiting
for the gray cloak of winter

and of grief
to ease...

freeing my shoulders,
unburdening the breath.

Afternoon stretches
into evening

leaving, overhead,
a web of lace.

The blue shows through.

Deborah Cooper

Spruce Swamp Sunset

Pink ribbons
shuttle through loose grey clouds
to weave a sunset,

interlacing tiny mouse tracks,
nubby hillocks of deer prints,
fleeting purple shadows of the owl.

Between spruce branches,
under the snow,
through mist and the weft of birdsong,
above our footprints,

silence.

Anne Simpson

Directions

First you'll come to the end of the freeway.
Then it's not so much north on Woodland Avenue
as it is a feeling that the pines are taller and weigh more,
and the road, you'll notice,
is older with faded lines and unmown shoulders.
You'll see a cemetery on your right
and another later on your left.
Sobered, drive on.
Drive on for miles
if the fields are full of hawkweed and daisies.
Sometimes a spotted horse
will gallop along the fence. Sometimes you'll see
a hawk circling, sometimes a vulture.
You'll cross the river many times
over smaller and smaller bridges.
You'll know when you're close;
people always say they have a sudden sensation
that the horizon, which was always far ahead,
is now directly behind them.
At this point you may want to park
and proceed on foot, or even
on your knees.

Connie Wanek

Poetry Group

His poetry hums as mellow as well
Oiled, warmed walnut walls, a lit, dignified
Fireplace, surrounded by oaken bookshelves
That chant with cello, wine and informed minds.
Her poetry sings in Finnish modern,
Packed with plaid shadows midst glitters of sun
Off churning water, full of rust by ferns,
Poems released on stone paths of ozone.
My poetry spits spiteful twitter,
Witty misery (choked humor), debris
That drowns in sounds and scenes of embittered
Ideas, blinded by ego and irony.
      A trio of blind mice, Northwoods seers,
      Stained angels, concocting poems for here.

Cal Benson

Night Work

In the dark time, surrounded by dreamers,
hovering over the warm smell of cut wood,
deft movements shaping lines of imagination
or caressing the cool surface one more time
with tender multi-nuanced strokes,
fingers stained by the blood of color,
inhaling the thick musk of inky silk,
gently touching the pristine surface
as it accepts contact with a sigh,
over and over again. the printer
pulls layer upon layer
of glowing transparent pleasure
into a subtly swelling echo
of the belovéd
Land.

Cecilia Lieder

About the Original Prints

The hand pulled prints reproduced here, which inspired the poetry in *Trail Guide*, are the works of artists of the Northern Printmakers Alliance. To see more prints by these printmakers, or to purchase one of the prints, go to <www.northernprintsgallery.com>

Title	Artist	Medium
A Time of Fire 76	Kurt Seaberg	Lithograph
American Suckers 42	Robb Quisling	Woodcut
At Woodbine Harbor 18	Matt Kania	Lithograph
Beaver with Branch 32	John Peyton	Lithograph
Bellows of Our Shared Breath 38	Nick Wroblewski	Woodcut
Black Bear on the Lakewalk 34	Matt Kania	Intaglio
Bunches of Blueberries 57	Sarah Angst	Linocut
Cackle of Crows 44	Sarah Angst	Linocut
Cascade Cabin 61	Joel Cooper	Screenprint
Chorus 78	Joe Furuseth	Woodcut
Compassion 66	Cecilia Lieder	Woodcut
Confession 70	Anna Marie Pavlik	Etching
Creek 7	Cecilia Lieder	Woodcut
Evening Sky on the North Shore 52	Ann Jenkins	Monoprint
Fiddleheads 25	Joel Moline	Wood Engraving
Isle Royale 46	Gendron Jensen	Lithograph
Magic Moment 51	Betsy Bowen	Woodcut
Magnetic Moment 49	Larry Basky	Screenprint
Midsummer 37	Jon Hinkel	Linocut
Midwinter's Evening 95	Jim Meyer	Woodcut
Most Unusual Clouds 21	Ann Jenkins	Monoprint
Potluck 90	Diane Chaney	Woodcut
Red-tailed Hawk 74	Alesa DeJager	Monoprint
Reflections on the Moon 92-3	Christine Herman	Monoprint
Regatta and Blue Horizon 15	Tom Rauschenfels	Woodcut
Reliquary 80	Anna Marie Pavlik	Etching
Shore 10	Alesa DeJager	Monoprint
Slough 13	Joel Cooper	Screenprint
Split Rock 55	Joel Moline	Wood Engraving
Spruce Swamp Sunset 98	Tom Rauschenfels	Woodcut
Sumac 58	Gaylord Schanilec	Wood Engraving
Sunset on Hale Lake 41	Glenna Olson	Woodcut
Taking Off! 87	Beckie Prange	Woodcut
The Luminous Hour 85	Kurt Seaberg	Lithograph
Untitled 29	Robert Repinski	Mixed Media
Waters United 16	Earl Austin	Etching
West Entrance 64	Gordon Manary	Linocut
Winter Moon 88	Ann Jenkins	Monoprint

INDEX OF POETRY

102

WE ARE GRATEFUL TO THESE REGIONAL BUSINESSES
AND INDIVIDUALS WHOSE GENEROUS SUPPORT HAS
HELPED MAKE THIS BOOK POSSIBLE.

THE SCHOOL OF ARTS AND LETTERS
THE COLLEGE OF ST. SCHOLASTICA

NORTH SHORE BANK OF COMMERCE
P.O. BOX 16450 DULUTH, MN 55802

NEW SCENIC CAFE · 5461 NORTH SHORE DR
OPEN 11AM DAILY · SERVING LUNCH AND DINNER

WHOLE FOODS CO-OP · 610 E. 4TH ST · 728-0884

LAKE SUPERIOR WRITERS
FOR MEMBERSHIP INFORMATION: WWW.LAKESUPERIORWRITERS.ORG

VISITDULUTH.COM - OFFICIAL TRAVEL RESOURCE

IN MEMORY OF MURIEL SHIREY

THE LOFT LITERARY CENTER · WWW.LOFT.ORG

CASCADE LODGE & RESTAURANT
CASCADE@CASCADELODGEMN.COM
A CABIN AT CASCADE LODGE WAS THE INSPIRATION FOR THE COVER SCREENPRINT

◆ A GIFT FROM ROBERT C. ARCHER ◆

CALYX DESIGN & PUBLISHING 218.724.5212

PAT DAUGHERTY PROOFREADER 218.727.7478

CHRISTIE PRINTING COMPANY, DULUTH

AND A SPECIAL THANKS TO THESE ARTISTS AND POETS WHO
CONTRIBUTED IN EXTRAORDINARY WAYS TO THE SUCCESS OF THIS
BOOK: CECILIA LIEDER, CAL BENSON, SHEILA PACKA, GARY BOELHOWER,
ANN NIEDRINGHAUS, ANNA MARIE PAVLIK, ANNE SIMPSON, MATT
KANIA, ELLIE SCHOENFELD, BETSY BOWEN, JOEL AND DEBORAH COOPER,
LISA POJE ANGELOS, MARK MAIRE, PAMELA MITTLEFEHLDT,
AND PAT DAUGHERTY.